New York
the Empire State

New York the Empire State

Photography by
Barry Kaplan

Introduction by
Hugh Carey

SKYLINE
PRESS

Special thanks are due to Peggy R. Bendel and the New
York State Department of Commerce for their help with
this project and to Linda Susan Serman Fuld for her
invaluable support and encouragement.
B.K.

Produced by Roger Boulton Publishing Services, Toronto
Designed by Fortunato Aglialoro
©1984 Oxford University Press (Canadian Branch)
SKYLINE PRESS is a registered imprint of
Oxford University Press

ISBN 0-19-540612-5
1 2 3 4 – 7 6 5 4

Printed in Hong Kong by Scanner Art Services, Inc., Toronto

INTRODUCTION

Prolonged exposure to the people and places of New York may induce contagious admiration, and extended contact with the history, the legends, the epochal evolution of The Empire State, and its residents, could well cause one to lapse into the constant superlative. As a New Yorker for life I conclude it is not just that the whole world is in New York, the entire universe is either here or on its way. This reflex is neither unique nor without precedent.

Two hundred years ago, in 1784, General George Washington, the Virginian who 'could not tell a lie', embarked upon a tour of New York. Of course he knew its heroic battlegrounds of Oriskany and Saratoga (the turning point of the Revolution); nor could he forget the Battle of Long Island, fought upon the heights and hills of Brooklyn. The Father of our Country was surveying the land of America for the foundation of the first capital of the new Republic. After sighting the harbors and ports, waterways and verdant countryside, mountainous watersheds and fertile valleys, George Washington prophesied that New York would become 'the seat of Empire'. In partial fulfilment of that prediction, on 30 April 1789 Washington stood with Robert Livingston, Chancellor of New York State, on the open balcony of the old City Hall on Wall Street and took his oath as President with the words 'So help me God'. He took his oath not as an Emperor. He had spurned the title of King for the higher calling of President of the Republic. One hundred and eighty years previously Henry Hudson had sailed past the Indian settlement of Manna-hata. Now New York was the first capital of the United States.

Though no longer the seat of national government, New York still bears the sobriquet 'The Empire State'. As we enter our third century, some observe that New York's diadem is tarnished, that her leadership among her sister states is faltering, and that her future is less promising than Washington's prophetic vision. In truth, other states and regions are and may become more populous but it is equally certain that no center of population possesses greater blessings and riches of diversity and pluralism than the Empire State. She has welcomed her sons and daughters as colonists and settlers and has given a home to impoverished and suffering immigrants. She is now and ever will be the first, best refuge of oppressed and abused human beings from all over the earth. Their shared diversity of race, creed and origin, often mindful of common adversity, endows New Yorkers with a special stamina. They pull together in times of stress like the strands of a drawn-steel cable bonded together to bear any burden. That element of shared strength is an assurance without arrogance that New Yorkers, regardless of census counts, will provide a fair share of leadership in whatever challenges lie ahead.

In facing the challenge of leadership in the coming century other states are now more massive but none is more strategic in site than the Gateway Corridor of New York. It is the only American state that faces both the Atlantic Ocean and the Great Lakes and it offers not one but two Great Lakes, Erie and Ontario. This key causeway to inner America stretches from Montauk Point along the 'water-level route' to Buffalo and Niagara Falls. The god-given feature of a natural concourse into the continental interior was a major boon to the communications and development of the Infant State and of its neighbors to the west but there is perhaps no more critical evidence of the zeal of New Yorkers to employ and improve their skills and their situation than their great exploits in this corridor.

They determined, with primitive means and manual labor, to build the Erie Canal, 363 miles of excavations and construction of locks and channels to link the Hudson River with Lake Erie. When Governor DeWitt Clinton opened the Canal in 1825, it was the climax to fifteen years of effort and the expenditure of 7 million dollars. While the opening of the Canal to barge traffic and travel was of great significance in itself it also heralded a development of even greater consequence, the human wave of European immigrants that brought five million New Yorkers into their new homeland between 1812 and 1860.

The Irish fleeing famine and persecution were joined by Germans who had been unsettled by political disorder. By 1880 millions of Italians arrived, displaced as farmers from their land, and these were joined by hundreds of thousands of Polish and Jewish victims of oppression coming from Russia and Eastern Europe.

The hundred and fifty years that followed the opening of the Erie Canal witnessed a symbiotic development of the State. While the Metropolitan New York City area grew as the new world center of trade, finance and industry, the immigrants joined the settlers in the Hudson-Erie Corridor in the creation of New York's major agricultural industry and of the mills and factories of the industrial revolution. Villages became hubs of industry and developed into the center cities of Albany, Rome, Utica, Syracuse, Rochester, and Buffalo.

The growth of New York's economy over that century and a half was such that the Empire State emerged as a world economic power. In fact, it has been estimated that, were New York a separate and independent nation, it would rank ninth in gross national product among modern countries. If all New York sought to be was an economic empire it had indeed succeeded. But the mainstay of the State is a less visible though more vital empire—a compendium of spiritual development, of human service and sacrifice. The spires and domes of churches and temples are picturesque and striking in their architectural variety. Gothic, Byzantine, colonial, and contemporary structures stand in villages and cities all over the State. The congregations that built these places of worship provide New York with a spiritual dimension, a voluntary sector that is shared by all faiths. It is that dimension which moved the political and social institutions of New York to develop a public and private partnership. That partnership has provided New York with the nation's most extensive and advanced system of serving the needs of exceptional people. In New York the severely disabled receive as much care and attention as is given to the superbly gifted. For instance, there are now over 800 family-type residences across the State for victims of cerebral palsy and developmentally disabled children and adults. They are manned by professionals and volunteers and are supported by public and private resources. It is this partnership, governmental and independent, public and private, which is common to many areas of human development in the State. Our great system of universities and colleges comprises State and City Universities and private and independent colleges. The financial commitment of New York to higher education, public and private, exceeds that of any other state and is larger than the entire federal subvention to higher education.

New York could point to a study that shows it has 36,000 millionaires, the largest number in America, but it means more to say that New York has emerged as a world center of health research and life-saving technology, with institutions like Sloan Kettering and Columbia Presbyterian in New York City, Roswell Park in Buffalo, and the Jones Cellular Research Center at Lake Placid.

In terms of the ultimate human sacrifice, New York has seen her most valiant men and women give their lives to defend the Republic in every engagement since the Revolution. There are memorials of their valor everywhere, from the statue of Father Duffy, Chaplain of the 'Fighting 69th', in Times Square, to the modest epitaphs in every village center and town common throughout the State.

The spiritual dimension of New York can be contemplated as pervasive and entire. To enjoy and understand the State physically it is best to see it region by region in all its beauty and variety. Starting from North to South, the high points of New York are its Adirondack Mountains. These are six million acres of 'purple mountain majesty' with 42 peaks higher than 4000 feet. Here are thousands of crystal-clear lakes, teeming with trout. Preserved 'forever wild' is the Adirondacks Park with campsites and hiking trails and ski slopes. Lake Placid, the site of the 1980 Olympics, where the US Hockey team defeated the Soviet Union on a goal by Mike Erazione, is perhaps best known for its resorts; but a tiny coulee, a serene pond, is the source of the mighty Hudson River high on Mount Marcy. That river and its tributaries cut scenic gorges of white water and rapids that meander and roar south to the navigable Hudson.

The Hudson is more than a great river. DeToqueville said, '—it is not a river, it is the center of the world.' The Indians called it 'the river that flows both ways', since it is an estuary, where the tidal action of the Atlantic reaches 100 miles from the river-mouth in New York Harbor.

At every bend in the river a page of history unfolds or a museum or a festival is to be seen. It passes the great Saratoga spa, summer home of the New York City Ballet and mecca of thoroughbred racing every August. The Empire State Capitol at Albany, with its monumental Mall, towers over the river as it moves south. As the Hudson nears the United States Military Academy at West Point it touches the birthplaces of Presidents Franklin D. Roosevelt and Martin Van Buren. At Highlands on the Hudson one of New York's many vineyards, Benmarl, is located. The new developments in winemaking have spread vineyards from Southold on the north fork of Long Island all the way to Chautaqua on Lake Erie. In some such as Benmarl one can own his own vine and claim his own vintage by name. The southerly course of the Hudson brings it past the land of Rip Van Winkle into Sleepy Hollow and the source of the legend of Washington Irving. The magnificent Palisades escort the Hudson to its wide lowlands at Tappan Zee.

To the credit of today's New Yorkers the river is cleaner now than decades ago. Strict laws protect it from contamination and the State has initiated major measures to end its endangerment from pollution.

West of the Hudson through the Valley of the Mohawk lies Cooperstown, the setting of James Fenimore Cooper's 'Leatherstocking' tales and more—it is the site of baseball's Hall of Fame and other museums of farming and folk art.

The Finger Lakes are six slender lakes brimming with salmon, trout and bass. Lake Seneca and its sisters are nestled in hills that resemble Alsace-Lorraine, and Hammondsport in the center of the wine country of New York has many French immigrants.

All the way west the Erie-Niagara frontier begins in Buffalo, New York's Gateway City of the West, a renascent city with an all-new rail system and a reborn downtown. Buffalo should be known as the Indomitable City. When it was nearly buried in the blizzard of 1977, its citizens reacted heroically to rescue their neighbors and averted a disaster.

Most accessible of the world's most majestic waterfalls, Niagara is more than a honeymoon center. The Native American Arts Center is a showcase for crafts that are unique and authentic to the American Indians.

Continuing north and east to the other end of Lake Ontario on the Canadian border we reach the Seaway Trail. Here between Oswego and Messina along the St Lawrence Seaway are the Thousand Islands, and the historic battlefields of the War of 1812, at Sacketts Harbor and Ogdensburg.

Southward bound from the Canadian border we travel through the Champlain Valley and Lake George Country down the Hudson again into the Catskill Mountain region. Here lies the resource which is at the heart of the Empire State's abundance. Orchards and dairylands, the black soil of onion farms, tall corn and tomatoes, make up an agricultural industry worth 2.6 billion dollars. The mainstay of that vital industry is not only New York's climate, soil and the skill of its farmers. A nearly unlimited and unspoiled supply of water has been secured in New York by an historic commitment on the part of its people. Manmade reservoirs in the Catskill region such as the Ashocan and Croton

Dam areas guard against the flooding of farmlands. Through a masterwork of planning and engineering, for nearly a century the water supply of New York City has been drawn from the lakes and rivers of the Catskills, another aspect of wonder in the Empire State.

The inns and hotels of the Catskill region are the epitome of upstate New York hospitality. Delectable food at affordable prices, recreation, entertainment, sports and athletic ethnic festivals all combine to bring families from all over the region and from New York City back to the old inns and front porches year after year.

We began by recalling that New York City was the nation's first capital. I believe that in the decades to come the city will be the financial capital and the leading international city in the world. After nearly collapsing financially ten years ago, New York City has experienced a remarkable and lasting recovery. As a center of financial and informational services, New York City has added nearly 500,000 employees to its work force. The entire transportation system is undergoing an overhaul backed by a commitment from New York State of 9 billion dollars. The City is experiencing a building boom unlike that of any other metropolis in the world. The redevelopment of whole areas such as Battery Park, the World Financial center, the South Street Seaport, the world's largest convention center and Times Square are underway. In the older neighborhoods there is a rehabilitation and an upgrading of the outer boroughs of Brooklyn, Queens and the Bronx.

It is not these material and structural signs alone that portend progress. Institutionally the cultural centers are strong. The Metropolitan Opera is one hundred years old and the Museum of Modern Art, now in its new home, is fifty years old and both are financially secure. All of the other cultural cousins are robust. The New York City and American Ballet, theatre off-Broadway, the Metropolitan Museum and the scores of art museums are all thriving. Some of this is thanks to tourism and the 'I Love New York' Program we started in 1977 to lift the morale of New York after near financial disaster, but I firmly believe that the undergirding of New York's future well-being is in the arrival not only of tourists but a surge of new Americans. As happened two hundred years ago with Northern Europeans, so now immigrants who are Asian, Hispanic and West Indian bring a new dynamic to New York. Their desire for education and self-improvement gives a new impetus toward a better society.

The story of New York the Empire State should close where the story of early New York began. Settlement of New York first took place on

Eastern Long Island. That salient, stretching 125 miles into the Atlantic Ocean, ends at Montauk Point. The Indians called that fork Eagles Neck. Stretching along the Atlantic shores on the south are the world's longest and most beautiful ocean beaches. Inland between the South and North Forks of Long Island are farmlands and now vineyards. More than 470 species of fish can be found in the waters of Long Island. Industry and advanced technology are burgeoning on the Island.

Long Island was the birthplace of New York's poet laureate Walt Whitman. His words from 'Leaves of Grass', written in 1855, portray those qualities that made New York and secure to New York its well-deserved title, 'The Empire State':

'...Here is not merely a nation but a teeming nation of nations. Here is action untied from strings.... Here is the hospitality which forever indicates heroes.... Here are the roughs and beards and space and ruggedness and nonchalance that the soul loves. Here the performance disdaining the trivial.... One sees it must indeed own the riches of the summer and winter, and need never be bankrupt while corn grows from the ground or the orchards drop apples or the bays contain fish or men beget children upon women.'

HUGH L. CAREY
New York, June 1984

1 Hot-air balloon over Glens Falls

2 The Staten Island Ferry (Fare 25¢)

3 Verrazano-Narrows Bridge between
Brooklyn and Staten Island, New York
City

4 *(left)* Country road, Allegany Region near Salamanca

5 Sunday afternoon, Hague, near Lake George

6 Historical marker near Fort Ann

7 Old cemetery, Fort Ann

8 The Clinton Academy, East Hampton, Long Island, established 1784
and now a museum

9 *(right)* Settlers' Monument, Lake George Village

10 The Benmarl Vineyards in the Hudson Valley, Marlboro

11 *(right)* Harvest Faun, Benmarl Vineyards

12 *(left)* Farmhouse, Thurman,
Adirondack Region

13 Local beauty, Florida

14 Fort Edward Historical Society Museum, Fort Edward

15 Warrensburg

16 Summer fair at Pepsico, Purchase, Westchester County

17 *(right)* Tending the garden, Stoney Creek

18 *(left)* Hague

19 Saturday afternoon at
Baskin-Robbins, Pelham Manor

20 *(left)* Street fair on Park Avenue South, New York City

21 Columbia University Campus, New York City

22 Ironville

23 Saint Mary's Star Of The Sea
Church, Brooklyn

24 *(left)* Holy Trinity Monastery, founded by Russian immigrants in
1930, Jordanville

25 The grounds-keeper at Holy Trinity Monastery

26 Diamond Point Post Office on Lake George

27 *(right)* Central Park, New York City

28 Antique shop, East Hampton, Long Island

29 Card game at Fleischmanns, an old resort town in the Catskills

30 Dairy farm, Chester, Orange County

31 *(right)* Southampton, Long Island

32 Old Champlain Canal Locks near Fort Edward

33 *(right)* Shrine to Albert Rudolph, Big Indian, Catskills

34 *(left)* Onion fields, Florida, 'onion capital of the world'

35 Raking hay, Wevertown, Adirondacks Region

36 New Windsor near Binghampton

37 Adirondack farmlands near Plattsburgh

38 Lake George

39 *(right)* Fishing boat off Montauk Point

40 Fenimore House, State Museum in Cooperstown, built on the site of
James Fenimore Cooper's home

41 *(right)* Saratoga Spa State Park, Saratoga Springs

42 *(left)* Syracuse

43 Altar boy, New Rochelle

44 Columbia University Campus, New York City

45 'The Sand Lot Kid' at the Baseball
Hall Of Fame, Cooperstown

46 The Hudson River in the Adirondacks, near Chestertown

47 Fishing in Prospect Park, Brooklyn

48 *(left)* Honor Roll, Thurman

49 Civil War memorial at the foot of
Mt Defiance, Ticonderoga

50 *(left)* 'Home Sweet Home' Museum, East Hampton, Long Island

51 Old Court House, Goshen

52 Hallowe'en, Warrensburg

53 'Haunted House' near Garnet Lake

54 *(left)* New York State Senate Chambers, State Capitol Building,
Albany

55 New York State Capitol Building, seen from the Empire State Plaza,
Albany

56 Sunday afternoon, North Creek

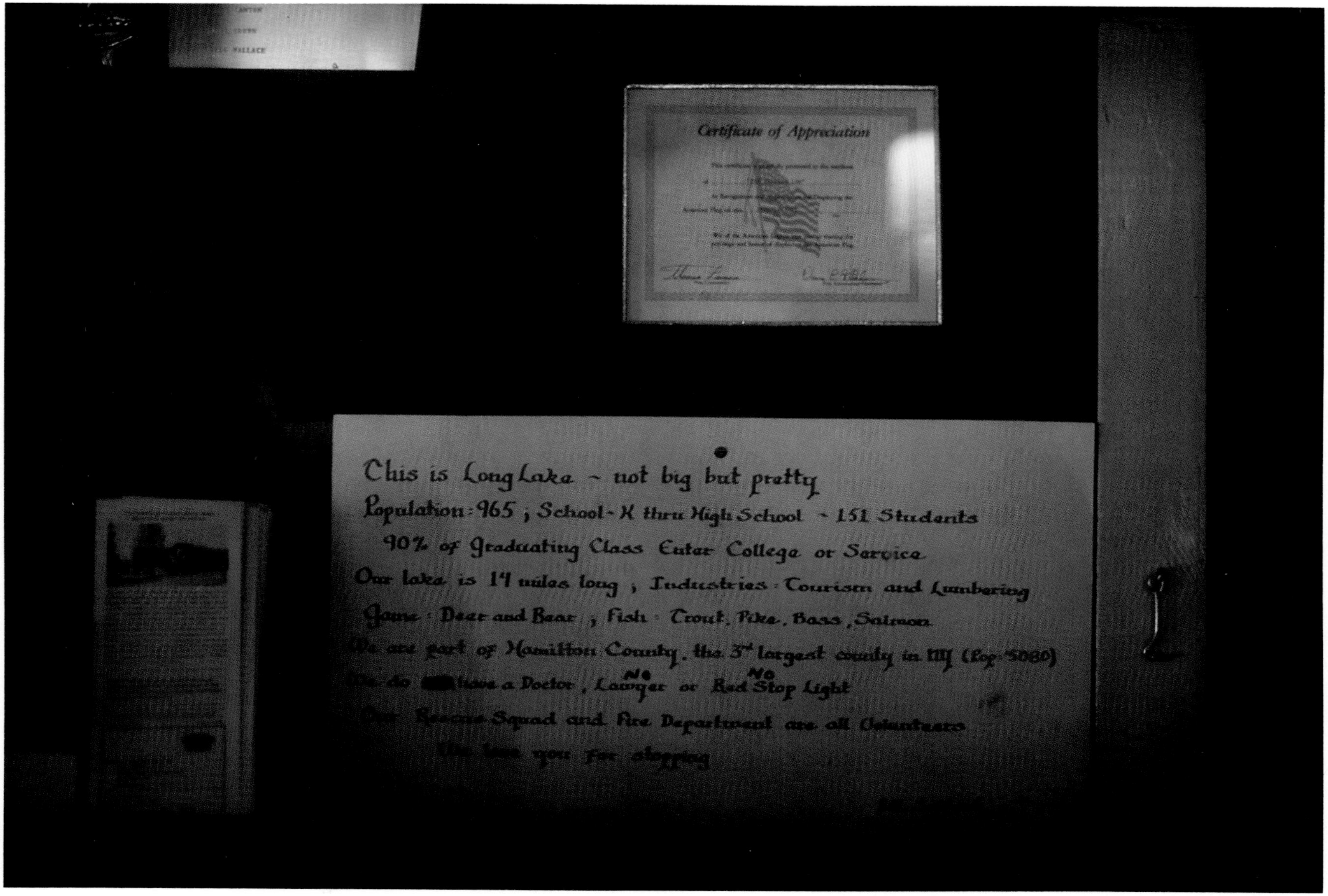

57 Bulletin board, Long Lake

58 Ashokan Reservoir, Shokan

59 *(right)* Autumn foliage, Rye

60 Edge of Sleepy Hollow Cemetery, burial place of Washington Irving, Terrytown

61 *(right)* Catskills near Fishs Eddy

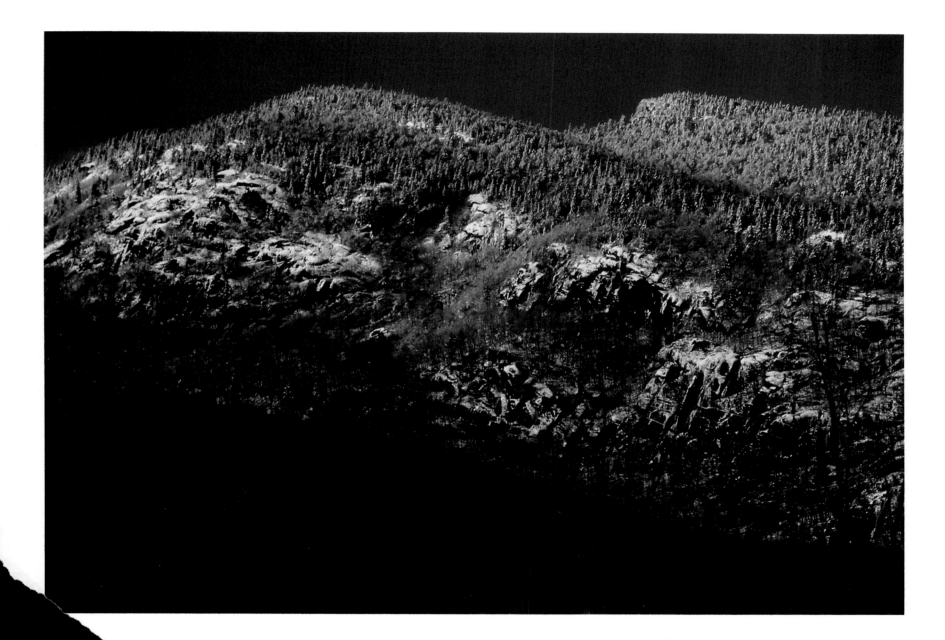

ing in winter, Pelham Manor

Mountains

64 Winter snowstorm, Ithaca

62 *(left)* Sledd﹍

63 Adirondack ﹍ersity, Ithaca

66 Horse farm, Walden

67 *(right)* Spring in Central Park, New York City

68 *(left)* Maple sugaring, Thurman

69 Sackets Harbor Battlefield, site of major battles in the war of 1812

70 Michael Boylan, blacksmith and horsebreeder, Katona

71 *(right)* Farmer, Baggs Coors, Thousand Islands—Seaway Region

72 *(left)* Main Street, Fleischmanns

73 Ferry to Vermont across Lake Champlain, near Ticonderoga

74 *(left)* United States Military Academy, founded 1802, West Point

75 Town Square, Ticonderoga

76 Lower Manhattan skyline, New York City

77 Syracuse, early morning

78 *(left)* Chinese New Year, Chinatown, New York City

79 Union Square, New York City

80 *(left)* Brooklyn Bridge, New York City

81 Niagara Falls

82 Sunset on Conesus Lake, Finger Lakes Region, near Livonia

83 One of the 'Thousand Islands' on the St Lawrence (there are actually more than 1800 in number)

84 *(left)* Farmers market, Long Island

85 Country road, Chester

86 Hudson River near Bear Mountain

87 *(right)* Balloon festival held every September in Queensbury near Glens Falls

88 Lighthouse at Montauk Point, tip of Long Island